Course Description:

This course is designed for managers who want to learn how to optimize the hiring process and recruit top talent quickly using the Sprint Recruiting methodology. Participants will learn how to streamline recruitment processes, engage with candidates effectively, and build a strong talent pipeline to meet business objectives.

Course Outline:

Introduction

Sprint Recruiting is an approach to recruiting and talent acquisition that enables organizations to find, hire, and onboard top talent in a fraction of the time and cost of traditional recruitment methods. It focuses on creating a well-defined and efficient process that aligns with organizational goals.

What is the importance of your recruiting process using the Agile Methodology?

The agile recruitment process enables organizations to quickly identify top talent, providing a competitive edge in the industry. It emphasizes collaboration and communication between all stakeholders, ensuring that everyone is on the same page throughout the hiring process. Sprint Recruiting works within a shorter timeline than traditional recruitment methods, enabling organizations to make decisions quicker and fill positions faster.

Overview of Sprint Recruiting

When it comes to hiring the right talent, there are numerous factors that need to be considered. From skills and experience to cultural fit and personality, finding the right candidate can be a daunting task. Sprint Recruiting gives you the benefits of a more flexible and iterative approach to recruitment.

Sprint Recruiting is an approach that takes its inspiration from the principles of agile software development. It involves breaking down recruitment into smaller, more manageable chunks, and focusing on collaboration and continuous improvement. The aim is to create a more dynamic and responsive recruitment process that can adapt to changing business needs and candidate requirements.

Implementing Sprint Recruiting in Your Organization

Implementing an agile approach to recruitment requires a specific set of skills and resources. However, with the right approach, it is possible to successfully embed an agile recruitment process in your organization.

The first step in implementing Sprint Recruiting is to assess your current recruitment process. This involves identifying areas where the process can be streamlined or improved, and determining where agile principles can be applied. It may also involve conducting a gap analysis to identify any areas where you may need additional resources or skills.

For example, you may find that your current recruitment process is slow and cumbersome, with too many stages and too many people involved. By streamlining the process and adopting agile principles, you can reduce the time-to-hire and ensure that you are attracting the right talent for your organization.

Building a Sprint Recruiting team involves bringing together a diverse group of people with different skills and perspectives. This could include HR professionals, hiring managers, team leaders, and subject matter experts. The aim is to create a team that can work collaboratively to identify and attract the right talent.

It is important to ensure that everyone on the team understands the agile approach and is committed to working together to achieve the shared goal of hiring the best talent for the organization. This may involve providing training and support to team members who are new to agile methodologies.

Establishing Sprint Recruiting Metrics and Goals

Establishing metrics and goals is essential for measuring the success of your Sprint Recruiting process. Metrics might include time-to-hire, cost-per-hire, or candidate satisfaction. Goals might include increasing the diversity of your workforce or reducing turnover rates. By establishing these metrics and goals, you can track progress and identify areas where improvements can be made.

For example, if your goal is to increase the diversity of your workforce, you might set a target for the percentage of hires from underrepresented groups. You can then track your progress against this target and make adjustments to your recruitment process as needed.

Overall, implementing Sprint Recruiting in your organization can help you to attract and hire the best talent more efficiently and effectively. By assessing your current recruitment process, building a Sprint Recruiting team, and establishing metrics and goals, you can ensure that your organization is well-positioned to compete for top talent in today's fast-paced and dynamic job market.

Sprint Recruiting Tools and Techniques

There are several tools and techniques that can be used to optimize the Sprint Recruiting process. These include:

Collaborative Hiring and Cross-Functional Teams

Collaborative hiring involves creating a team of people from different departments or disciplines who can work together to identify and assess candidates. By bringing together a diverse group of people, you can get a more holistic view of each candidate and make more informed hiring decisions.

Continuous Improvement and Feedback Loops

Continuous improvement involves analyzing feedback from candidates, new hires, and hiring managers to identify areas where the recruitment process can be improved. Feedback loops allow you to collect this feedback on a regular basis and use it to make ongoing improvements.

Leveraging Technology for Sprint Recruiting

Technology can be used to automate many aspects of the recruitment process, such as resume screening and scheduling interviews. Additionally, technology can help to create a more streamlined and efficient recruitment process, which can help to reduce time-to-hire and improve the overall candidate experience.

Balancing Speed and Quality in the Hiring Process

Sprint Recruiting can prioritize speed over quality, which can lead to making the wrong hiring decisions or not attracting the best talent. It is important to find a balance between speed and quality to ensure that you are hiring the best candidates.

The Bottom Line

Sprint Recruiting is a flexible and iterative approach to recruitment that can help organizations to identify and attract the right talent quickly and efficiently. By implementing agile principles and using the right tools and techniques, organizations can create a more dynamic and responsive recruitment process that can adapt to changing business needs and candidate requirements.

While there are challenges associated with Sprint Recruiting, the benefits of adopting this approach make it an attractive option for organizations looking to improve the quality and speed of their recruitment processes.

Selling Sprint Recruiting to your organization

There are some key benefits to market as you begin selling the concept of Sprint Recruiting throughout your organization:

1. **More Control**: Incremental developments hold tremendous value for the project team and the customer. Work can be broken into parts and conducted in rapid, iterative cycles. The regular meetings that are part of agile allow project teams to share progress, discuss problems and work out solutions.

They also help make the entire process more transparent.

Sprint Recruiting provides the team with early visibility of the majority of potential problems, allowing project teams to proactively address them before they become serious issues further down the line. By breaking down a complex process into smaller pieces and taking ownership for each part, teams are able to better allocate the required resources to accomplish the sprint goals and forecast the ability to achieve results within the sprint.

Sprint Recruiting eliminates chaos from the recruitment process by providing a structured system that ensures clarity among recruiters and candidates alike, creating mutual accountability throughout the entire hiring cycle.

2. **Higher Quality and Productivity**: The incremental nature of the agile method means that projects are completed in shorter sprints, making them more manageable. It also allows products to be rolled out quickly and changes to be easily made at any point during the process. This boosts the team's productivity, as tasks are completed within shorter timelines.

The methodology encourages teams to think outside the box and develop creative solutions to problems. This helps reduce the amount of time spent on mundane tasks, allowing project teams to focus on more important work that requires their attention. Sprint Recruiting is also a great way for organizations to streamline the recruitment process and find top talent quickly. The shorter cycle times mean fewer resources are needed for recruiting, which leads to a decrease in overall costs.

The Sprint Recruiting Methodology helps create a more collaborative work environment. Teams can easily communicate and collaborate with one another on tasks and projects during sprints, allowing them to get more done in less time. This also leads to improved quality and fewer delays due to miscommunication or lack of planning.

Because it is iterative, one big benefit of agile methodology is the ability to find problems and create solutions quickly and efficiently. The flexibility of the methodology allows project teams to respond to customer reaction and constantly improve the product.

3. **Higher Customer Satisfaction**: Close collaboration between the recruiting team and the customer provides immediate feedback. The customer is able to make tweaks to their expectations and desires throughout the process. The result: a more satisfied customer.

Your clients set the prioritization of the recruiting work for the sprint. This provides the client the control to dictate how your team spends its time, aligning to the goals of the company first. Agile methodology encourages an open dialog between the customer and the team to ensure everyone is on the same page.

With Sprint Recruiting, processes are streamlined to reduce unnecessary steps, resulting in improved velocity and quality of work. It helps create a continuous cycle of improvement that can be implemented throughout your organization. Additionally, it encourages better communication and collaboration between team members, resulting in more efficient processes and higher quality output.

Sprint Recruiting helps to optimize the hiring process by streamlining the recruitment process and identifying the best candidates quickly. By breaking the recruitment process into smaller parts, teams are able to optimize their resources and time to ensure successful outcomes.
Sprint Recruiting creates a better process, aligned to the client, increases speed and velocity without sacrificing the quality of hire. All are components to what increases client satisfaction.

4. **Higher Return on Investment:** The agile method's iterative nature also means the end product is ready for market faster, staying ahead of the competition and quickly reaping benefits. The benefits of the agile method are cutting costs and time to market in half, while increasing application quality and customer satisfaction.

Sprint Recruiting helps to reduce the cost of recruitment and onboarding by enabling organizations to hire faster, with fewer resources. It also allows teams to shift focus from recruiting to other areas of their business, freeing up time and money that can be invested elsewhere.

5. **Sanity**: Before Sprint Recruiting, I felt like a boat without a rudder, being pushed into whichever direction my stakeholders decided. I have now implemented Sprint Recruiting in at least three different companies, and I feel more empowered to lead my team. I have the data I need to make the necessary decisions to move my organization forward and capture the top talent in my industry.

My team members are empowered to make decisions to directly affect the course of our recruiting organization. Each of us works more closely with our hiring managers as hiring partners, and we no longer see them as adversaries. In fact, engagement levels of recruiters, hiring managers, and even candidates have increased, and we are able to respond faster to market changes than many of our competitors.

In this course, you will learn all the steps that took me years to develop so that you can implement them and gain the benefits immediately. You will learn what the problems are in modern-day recruiting, how Sprint Recruiting can help solve these problems, and how you can implement Sprint Recruiting to reap the same benefits that we've been seeing.

If you would like a free presentation outlining the benefits above to present to leadership, click https://sprintrecruiting.files.wordpress.com/2023/04/the-benefits-of-sprint-recruiting-.pdf.

Understanding Sprint Recruiting

- Key principles of Sprint Recruiting
- How it differs from traditional recruitment methods
- Creating a culture that failure is ok

Key principles of Sprint Recruiting

Here's a quick reminder of the 4 Dysfunctions and 4 Principles of Sprint Recruiting:

Sprint Recruiting 2021

The 4 Dysfunctions of Normal Recruiting

- EVERYTHING IS A PRIORITY WHICH MEANS NOTHING IS A PRIORITY
- IT LACKS A RHYTHM AND OPPORTUNITY FOR ITERATIVE IMPROVEMENT
- CLIENTS AND RECRUITERS ARE OFTEN MISALIGNED ON DEFINITION OF SUCCESS
- THE FEEDBACK LOOP IS BROKEN

The 4 Principles of Sprint Recruiting

- THE **SPRINT** CREATES **EFFICIENCIES**
- THE **BUSINESS** DEFINES **PRIORITY**
- **WORK IN PROGRESS LIMITS** CREATE **FOCUS** AND **ITERATIVE EFFICIENCY**
- **FEEDBACK** KEEPS THE PROCESS **MOVING**

How it differs from traditional recruitment methods

1.   **Speed**: Sprint Recruiting is designed to move quickly, with a focus on identifying and hiring top candidates as quickly as

possible. Traditional recruiting methods can often be slower, with a longer time to fill and more complex processes.

2.   **Focus on quality over quantity:** Sprint Recruiting emphasizes the importance of finding the right candidate, rather than simply filling the role quickly. Traditional recruiting methods may prioritize volume over quality, resulting in a larger pool of candidates to choose from but potentially missing out on the best fit for the role.

3.   **Collaboration**: Sprint Recruiting places a strong emphasis on collaboration between the hiring team and the recruiter, with frequent communication and involvement from the hiring manager. Traditional recruiting methods may rely more on the recruiter alone to find and select candidates.

4.   **Personalized approach**: Sprint Recruiting seeks to build a personal connection with candidates, with a focus on engaging with a small number of highly qualified individuals in a meaningful way. Traditional recruiting methods may take a more impersonal approach, relying on job postings and online applications to attract candidates and then losing them in a laborious recruiting process.

5.   **Agile process**: Sprint Recruiting uses an agile methodology, which means that the hiring process can be adapted and refined as needed based on feedback and results. Traditional recruiting methods may rely on a more rigid process that is harder to change or adjust as needed.

One of the first steps to a successful implementation for Sprint Recruiting is to be sure you and your team have a growth mindset. You need to be open and willing to learn, experiment, and measure. The ability to fail and learn from these failures is essential for successful implementation.

You also need to commit to the process, and be dedicated to continual improvement. Sprint Recruiting isn't a magic bullet - if you want success, it needs constant attention and effort. Once you have the right mindset, you can begin planning the particular approaches that will work best for your organization.

You'll want to determine what goals are most important (quality vs quantity of hires), develop strategies for engaging with candidates in meaningful ways (such as utilizing technology or networking events), and find ways to measure effectiveness on an ongoing basis.

With these tools in hand, you can implement Sprint Recruiting effectively within your recruitment team, making sure everyone is onboard with the plan from start to finish. As you progress, be sure to monitor the results of your efforts, and continue to adjust and refine as needed. With this ongoing effort, you can make Sprint Recruiting work for your team.

Be sure to check out the Growth Mindset preparation form by clicking https://sprintrecruiting.files.wordpress.com/2023/04/sprint-recruitingleader-mindset-preparation.pdf.

Failure is the path to success

What has Sprint Recruiting Taught Me? Failure is directly linked to success!

As a HR professional or recruiter, you know how important it is to have successful hiring processes and recruit top talent. But have you ever stopped to think about the valuable lessons that failure can teach?

Let's take an honest look at failure's role in recruiting success and discuss why focusing on mistakes – as much as successes – can help identify areas of improvement.

Why failure is an important part of the recruitment process

When seeking new hires, interviewing and recruiting can be time-consuming processes. However, failure to recognize suitable employees can have a huge impact on businesses. Therefore it is important to view failure during the recruitment process as an invaluable learning experience rather than a hindrance.

Sprint Recruiting embraces the idea of failure. During our retrospective meetings, teams discuss what didn't work during the sprint. By sharing challenging experiences and analyzing what went wrong, teams can gain a better understanding of gaps in the recruitment process. This helps identify strengths, weaknesses, and opportunities for improvement that can be applied to future sprints.

Although it is important to learn from mistakes made during the recruiting process, it is also essential to use this knowledge to move forward. Sprint Recruiting encourages teams to constantly improve their recruitment strategies, resulting in successful hires and a more knowledgeable workforce. Companies should aim to use failures experienced during recruitment and track how the team overcame the obstacles to avoid in the future.

Strategies to keep in mind when dealing with failure

Dealing with failure can be a hectic process and not everyone has the same approach. However, there are several strategies you can keep in mind that will help you reflect on the occurrence and move forward.

Focusing on what you have gained from the experience, such as resilience or knowledge, can be a great way to feel empowered instead of discouraged. In every failure, there is a lesson to be learned for future sprints. It's also a great opportunity to identify the recurring obstacles that prevent your team from succeeding during the sprint.

When we were beta testing the Sprint Recruiting methodology, we only had three principles at the time. I noticed every sprint we did not meet the client's definition of success in terms of points won, there was a common theme: Hiring Manager feedback. It was this recurring obstacle that caused us to add the 48 hour feedback deadline to our principles. Had we not stopped and truly assessed why we failed, we would have continued to produce the same mistakes at the expense of our client's needs and the candidate's experience.

Also, don't forget to reward yourself for what is accomplished and realize that small steps are just as important as big ones.

The importance of learning from your mistakes and being resilient

Everyone makes mistakes, and it is important to recognize the importance of learning from them and not letting the fear of failing stop you from trying new things. Resilience is a key factor in achieving team goals, as it gives us the strength to keep pushing forward after failure or disappointment. It also allows us to remain optimistic despite challenges, as well as developing inner-strength necessary for success.

Failing and being resilient helps us explore our true potential and strive for something better. Learning from mistakes can give us wisdom and enlightenment not only about others, but ourselves too.

Sometimes, I find teams are afraid and almost adamantly opposed to admitting failure. But while it can be difficult to admit when you've made a mistake or failed, it is important to acknowledge the mistakes and discuss them openly. This allows us to identify what went wrong and make adjustments so that we can move ahead in a more positive direction.

It has always been important for me to recognize how learning from failure can help me become a more resilient problem-solver. I have found that when teams work together to find solutions and share their experiences, learning becomes easier and the team spirit grows stronger.

Tips for staying motivated during the recruitment process

Staying motivated and positive during a recruitment process can be challenging. It's important to create a routine that helps you push through any setbacks and maintain enthusiasm for your job search.

Start each day by reflecting on what you have already achieved, then set new goals for the day. Find ways to break down large tasks into smaller ones to make them more manageable - this will help keep you motivated and inspired. The essence of Sprint Recruiting is to allow recruiters visibility to the client's definition of success for the sprint and align their activities and focus to that definition. When you are able to gain this type of perspective, the impact of failure has a smaller effect.

I've worked with teams who failed and failed big during their first few sprints. This is normal but the teams quickly became unmotivated. When we shifted the conversation and focus to what we learned, the teams began to regain their confidence and perspective. Leaders must be aware of their team's tolerance for failure and the impacts it has on motivation.

Examples of successful people who used failure as a stepping stone to success

Many successful people have used failure as a stepping stone to success. For example, Steve Jobs experienced rejection and failure when he sold an early version of the Apple computer but that experience inspired him to create one of the most iconic companies of our time. J.K Rowling was famously rejected by a dozen publishers before her Harry Potter series became one of the best-selling book series in history.

Another prime example is Thomas Edison who famously said that "I have not failed 10,000 times - I've successfully found 10,000 ways that will not work." Edison's determination to find a way through failure and eventually create something revolutionary serves as an inspiring reminder that we all can overcome and use failure as a tool for growth and success.

Summary

While the job recruitment process can be full of challenges and difficulties, it is important to remember that failure is part of any journey. Don't be discouraged by defeats or rejection - instead, use them as learning opportunities. Remember to stay motivated throughout the process, that your ultimate success is determined by how you handle your failures. Reflect on them and use them to push yourself further.

The recruitment process isn't easy but with a positive outlook, dedication and determination, you will reach your goal. It all comes down to your mindset.

Prepare for Sprint Recruiting

- Identify your goals
- Building a strong recruitment team
- Defining roles and responsibilities
- Setting up a recruitment process that supports Sprint Recruiting
- Key steps in a typical Sprint Recruiting process

Here are some quick goals you will want to set for yourself and your team as you begin implementing Sprint Recruiting:

1. **Define the roles**: The first step of Sprint Recruiting is to clearly define the role of each participant in the process. This involves identifying the key responsibilities and required skills, as well as any specific qualifications or experience that are necessary for success in the role.

2. **Focus on quality over quantit**y: Sprint Recruiting emphasizes the importance of quality over quantity when it comes to candidates. Rather than casting a wide net and hoping to find the right person, Sprint Recruiting focuses on identifying a small number of highly qualified candidates and engaging with them in a personalized and meaningful way.

3. **Move quickly:** The third step of Sprint Recruiting is to move quickly throughout the hiring process. This involves setting clear timelines for each stage of the process and working efficiently to ensure that you don't lose top candidates to competitors.

4. **Involve the hiring managers**: Finally, Sprint Recruiting emphasizes the importance of involving the hiring manager throughout the process, especially for those roles assigned points. This involves ensuring that the hiring manager is actively involved in candidate screening and selection, and that they have a clear understanding of the hiring criteria, process and feedback expectations. By involving the hiring manager, Sprint Recruiting

aims to ensure that the candidate selected is the right fit for the team and the organization as a whole.

By following these four principles, you can ensure that you are successfully implementing Sprint Recruiting in your organization and setting yourself up for success. With this approach, you will be able to quickly identify the right candidates and move through the recruitment process efficiently, while also ensuring that all hiring decisions are based on quality over quantity.

Building a strong recruitment team

Recruiting top talent is one of the most important tasks for any business. That's why having a strong recruitment team in place is essential if you want to ensure that you're able to attract and retain the best candidates for your organization.

From understanding how to market positions effectively and create engaging candidate experiences, to mastering the evaluation process and tapping into new sources of potential applicants, there are many components involved in creating a successful recruitment team. In this section, we'll dive into these elements so that you can develop a well-rounded team primed for success.

Develop a competency model to assess the skills and experience of potential team members

Developing a competency model to assess the skills and experience of potential team members is a critical task for any organization. A competency model helps managers determine the ideal skills and experience mix for a particular team and assess candidate fit with those criteria. It can also help identify gaps in performance within an existing team, uncover training needs, and create job profiles which are used to match up potential candidates.

I like to use the WHO Interview model to develop my job descriptions and competency models for recruiting teams.

Mission: The mission is the essence of the job and should be an executive summary of the job's core purpose. *Example: To double revenue over three years by identifying and acquiring large profitable contracts with industrial customers.* Be as specific as possible for potential candidates to understand what will be expected of them at a high level.

Outcomes: What are the predetermined outcomes of the recruiter role for the first year or as a whole? Be sure to list at least 3, maximum of 5, outcomes expected from this role. These should be KPIs to determine the success of the candidate if hired into the role.

Examples could be:
1.   Develop an active and managed pipeline of software developer candidates for the greater bay area totaling a minimum of 100 qualified candidates.
2.   Create a candidate marketing strategy to include social media outreach, communication timelines and assessment of results
3.   Conduct at least four market visits to best determine recruiting efforts for key roles including developers, QA Engineers and DevOps candidates. Results to be presented within the first six months of hire.

By thoroughly answering these questions, you'll be able to create a robust competency model that will help you find the best possible recruitment team.

Competencies: Competencies define *how* you expect a new hire to operate in the fulfillment of the job and the achievement of the outcomes. I suggest a minimum of 3, maximum of 5, competencies from the list below (based on the list provided by the <u>WHO Interview book</u>):

1. **Analysis Skills**-Analytical skills refer to the ability to collect, analyze, and interpret complex data sets to understand patterns, identify problems, and develop insights. These skills involve critical thinking, attention to detail, and proficiency in data analysis tools and techniques.
2. **Brainpower/learns quickly-Learns quickly**- Demonstrates ability to quickly and proficiently understand and absorb new information.
3. **Creative/Innovative**-Generates new and innovative approaches to problems.
4. **Sets high standards and goals**-Intrinsically motivated by accomplishing target goals and both internally and externally competitive.
5. **Intelligence**-The ability to learn quickly, solve problems, and make good decisions.
6. **Aggressive**- Moves quickly and takes a forceful stand without being overly abrasive.
7. **Integrity**- honesty, ethics, and trustworthiness.
8. **Coachability**- Possess the willingness to listen to feedback and improve.
9. **Results Oriented**- Has the drive to achieve goals and produce results.
10. **Passion**- Exhibits enthusiasm and commitment to the job.
11. **Work ethic**- Thrives in their willingness to work hard and persevere through challenges.
12. **Teamwork**- Shows the ability to collaborate effectively with others.
13. **Emotional intelligence**- Exhibits the ability to understand and manage one's own emotions, as well as the emotions of others.
14. **Adaptability**- The ability to adjust to changing circumstances and new challenges.
15. **Communication**-Speaks and writes clearly and articulately without being overly verbose or talkative.

By exploring these competencies carefully, organizations can ensure they have the right candidates in place with the required skills to move forward successfully.

If you would like to see my template version of a Sprint Recruiter, please click https://sprintrecruiting.files.wordpress.com/2023/04/the-sprint-recruiter-job-profile.pdf.

Find recruiters with a growth mindset

For any business looking to grow its team, recruiters with a growth mindset are invaluable. They take an innovative approach to finding candidates, seeing beyond qualifications and skills alone to identify people with potential who can adapt and contribute to an evolving organizational structure. Recruiters with a growth mindset possess the right blend of networking and relationship building skills, pinpointing talent that has both current and future value.

Not only can they track down the best available options for open roles, but also provide insight on how filling those positions can shape the company's development strategies for the long term.

Recruiting leaders seeking lasting success would do well to invest in recruiters with a growth mindset. (Be sure to complete the mindset preparation on your team if you have not already done so.)

Find recruiters who have an entrepreneurial mindset

For businesses looking to diversify their team, recruiters who have an entrepreneurial mindset offer valuable insight and experience. They can help identify talented individuals who are suited for roles that require an independent approach with a drive to succeed. Recruiters with an entrepreneurial mindset are also well-versed in the latest technology, meaning they understand the needs of startups and more established businesses alike.

Here are some of the key characteristics of a recruiter with an entrepreneurial mindset:

1.   Creativity: An entrepreneurial recruiter must be creative in sourcing and attracting top talent. They need to think outside the box and develop new strategies to find the best candidates.

2.   Adaptability: Successful entrepreneurs are always adapting to changing circumstances and environments. A recruiter with an entrepreneurial mindset must be able to quickly pivot and adjust their approach to stay ahead of the competition.

3.   Results-driven: An entrepreneurial recruiter is focused on achieving results. They set clear goals and metrics, and continuously measure their success against these targets.

4.   Strong communication skills: Effective communication is crucial for building strong relationships with candidates and clients. A recruiter with an entrepreneurial mindset must be an excellent communicator, able to build rapport and establish trust quickly.

5.   Strategic thinking: An entrepreneurial recruiter must have strong strategic thinking skills. They need to be able to see the big picture, anticipate trends, and identify new opportunities for growth and expansion.

If you actively search out these types of recruiters, your organization will be able to benefit from having creatives on staff that think beyond the box and outside of current trends.

Create a thorough interview process to ensure you make the right hire

It is essential that businesses take the time to establish a comprehensive interview process for each position they seek to fill. This process should involve more than one interviewer, ideally those in higher positions such as team leaders or managers. Questions should be tailored to not only provide insight into a candidate's technical skills and experience, but their communication style and overall attitude. With this mindset, recruiting leaders will be able to identify how potential employees may fit into the existing culture of their company and complement the current team dynamic.

According to the book "Who: The A Method for Hiring" by Geoff Smart and Randy Street, the interview process involves the following steps:

1.   Phone screen: Conduct a brief phone interview with the top candidates to confirm their qualifications and assess their communication skills.

2.   First interview: Bring the top candidates in for an in-person interview with the interview team. Use a structured interview process to ensure that each candidate is evaluated consistently. Ask questions that are designed to elicit specific information about the candidate's past performance and behavior.

3.   Second interview: If necessary, bring the top candidates back for a second interview with the interview team. This interview should be more in-depth and may involve additional questions and assessments.

4.   Reference check: Conduct reference checks on the top candidate to verify their employment history, job performance, and character. This is a critical step in the process. Asking the references the following questions:

a.   What was the candidate hired to do?
b.   How well did they meet the expectations of the role?
c.   Why did they leave?

Use this information to compare to the answers the candidate provided you to the same questions to get to the truth of whether this candidate will be a good fit for your organization.

5.   Job offer: Once you have completed the interview process and reference checks, extend a job offer to the top candidate.

6.   The authors emphasize the importance of a structured and consistent interview process that focuses on assessing the candidate's skills, experience, and character. They also recommend using behavioral interviewing techniques to elicit specific examples of past behavior that demonstrate the candidate's ability to perform in the role. By following this process,

organizations can increase their chances of hiring the right person for the job.

One of the key interviews goes through the candidate's previous 3-5 employers requiring them to answer the following questions:
- What were you hired to do? Ask them to be specific including KPIs and metrics they were to achieve.
- How did you perform against your goals? Again, press for specifics. This is a huge indicator of whether the candidate will be successful in the role you have available.
- Why did you leave? Believe it or not, this is one of the most telling questions of the process. It will allow you to understand what motivates the candidate to leave. Do they leave when they don't get their way or are they only leaving to take on more responsibilities.

This interview method saved me from a hire I was about to make. After the first couple of interviews, I had made up my mind I had found the perfect recruiter candidate. They had the competencies and attitude I was looking for. The panel interview and I went through these three questions with the candidate as a final step. The last question proved to be invaluable as every time the candidate left a role, it was because they "disagreed with the new manager". This was the nail in the coffin for me and I continued to search for a recruiter more inline with the success model I had created for the role.

Also be sure to develop a model or bank of follow-up questions during an interview may help recruiters come to a decision on who might best suit the job in question. By outlining these parameters ahead of time, organizations will be better equipped to select the best potential hire with confidence.

Provide ongoing training and development for all recruitment team members

Perhaps one of the greatest recruiting leader malpractice behaviors is our lack of attention to the continuous development of our teams.

Offering ongoing training and development for all recruitment team members can ensure that everyone in the team is aware of key industry changes, as well as new regulations emerging out of the employment sector. Ensuring that each team member has the most up-to-date knowledge of developments within their field provides many rewards – from increasing efficiency to employee job satisfaction – ultimately leading to a more productive recruitment environment.

A culture of continuous learning creates a positive cycle where effective strategies are honed and employees feel supported in their development. It is essential to any modern recruitment department.

Setting up a recruitment process that supports Sprint Recruiting

One of the key steps of success for implementing Sprint Recruiting is setting up the process. When I consult companies, the first step I take is to conduct an analysis of the recruiting journey map.

A journey map is a tool used in design thinking to visually represent the steps and stages of a customer or user's experience with a product or service. It is a way to understand the user's needs, emotions, pain points, and overall satisfaction throughout their interaction with a particular product or service.

A journey map typically includes several key components, including:
1.   **Persona**: A representation of the user, often based on research and data, that includes demographic information, behaviors, and goals.
2.   **Timeline**: A chronological representation of the user's journey, often broken down into specific stages or phases.
3.   **Touchpoints**: Moments of interaction between the user and the product or service, including physical and digital interactions.
4.   **Emotions**: An exploration of the user's emotional state throughout the journey, including positive and negative emotions.
5.   **Pain points**: Areas of frustration or difficulty for the user during their journey.
By creating a journey map, you can gain a deeper understanding of the user's experience, identify areas for improvement, and ultimately create more effective and user-centered products and services.

The next step is to assess how Sprint Recruiting will assist in the pain points as well as enhance the praise points. This is a vital step in selling the methodology to your team and stakeholders. This will also serve as a process map for you to translate current processes against the new Sprint Recruiting model you will be implementing.

From this exercise, document the changes and provide the documentation in a central, easily accessible drive or virtual location for key stakeholders to access when needed.

Determine the length of your sprint

As a reminder from the book, the length of the sprint is completely up to the recruiting leader and their organization. Some helpful items to consider in the decision are:

1.   Recruiting needs: The number of positions to fill and the level of urgency for each position can help determine the length of the sprint.
2.   Availability of hiring team: The availability of the hiring team can impact the length of the sprint. If key decision-makers are unavailable for a certain period, it may be necessary to adjust the length of the sprint accordingly.
3.   Candidate availability: The availability of potential candidates can also impact the length of the sprint. If there is a limited pool of candidates, a shorter sprint may be necessary to ensure the best candidates are secured.
4.   Time to hire: The desired time to hire can also play a role in determining the length of the sprint. If there is a pressing need to fill positions quickly, a shorter sprint may be necessary.
5.   Complexity of positions: The complexity of the positions being recruited for can also impact the length of the sprint. More complex positions may require a longer sprint to allow for more thorough screening and evaluation of candidates.

Overall, the length of a sprint in Sprint Recruiting should be determined based on the specific needs and circumstances of the hiring organization, taking into account factors such as recruiting needs, candidate availability, and the desired time to hire.

My preference is two weeks because it breaks most months up into smaller pieces and is long enough to collect the needed data for iteration but short enough to remain adaptable and flexible.

Key Term: Definition of Done

In the Agile framework, a fundamental definition of what "Done" must be established. One of my favorite authors, Brene Brown, talks about the importance of a team definition when a project is complete. For her team, "paint done" creates space for input from all parties. It "unearths stealth expectations and unsaid intentions, and it gives the people charged with the task tons of color and context," she writes. "It fosters curiosity, learning, collaboration, reality-checking, and ultimately success."

Early in our beta version of Sprint Recruiting, we decided to define Done as when the candidate started. It seemed like the most straightforward, easy way to determine when we were done with a job in the Sprint, but it presented some data obstacles we did not think through. Our goal was to track the candidate journey's improvement, but some aspects of the onboarding process were outside of our control. We decided to redefine our definition to circumvent these obstacles and reclassify our Done to mean when the candidate accepts and signs the offer letter.

It may not seem like an important step, but I will caution you that skipping this step can prove detrimental to your implementation. Done's definition will be what your team and the client use to stop the clock on the sprint process so take the time to think through what works best for your team.

What is your definition of Done? Take time to write it below.

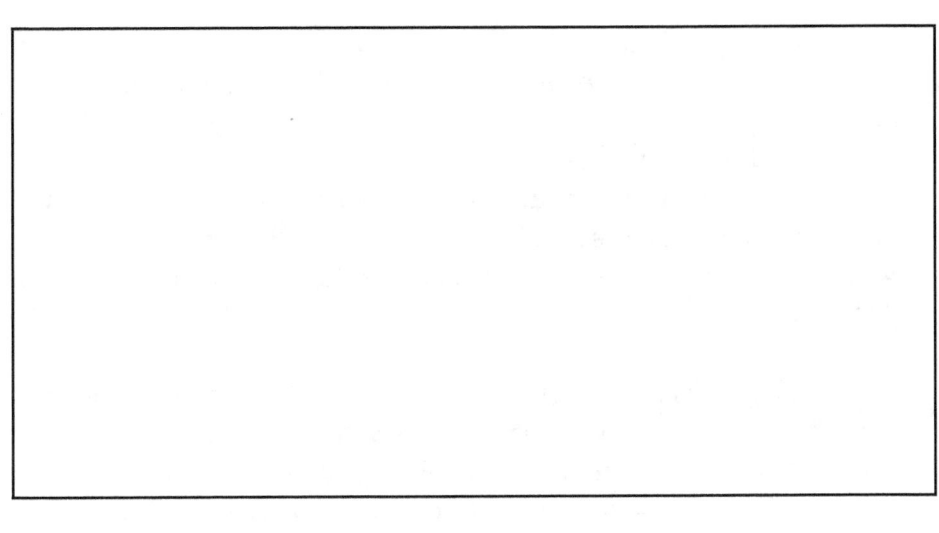

Determine your key players

Implementing Sprint Recruiting is a team effort so be sure to take the time to identify the key players in the process. Typically, this includes roles like the hiring managers, HR representatives, senior executives and recruiting specialists.

You also want to ensure that all of these key players have access to the same information in order to make sure everyone is on the same page when it comes to making decisions. Be sure to provide training for each team member on the process so that they understand their role and the objectives.

Let's review some of the key roles in the Sprint Recruiting Process.

Recruiting Leader

The recruiting leader in Sprint Recruiting serves the same role as the SCRUM Master in Agile. The Scrum Master is the team role responsible for ensuring the team lives Agile values and principles and follows the processes and practices that the group agreed they would use.
The responsibilities of this role include:

- Clearing obstacles
- Establishing an environment where the team can be effective
- Addressing team dynamics
- Ensuring a good relationship between the team and sprint owner as well as others outside the team
- Protecting the team from outside interruptions and distractions.

As the recruiting leader, you have to keep the team moving toward filling those assigned points during the Sprint. You will find your schedule more consumed with identifying and overcoming obstacles versus chasing fires as you would in traditional recruiting. You will also be responsible for facilitating the daily stand ups and retro meetings with your team throughout the sprint process. In some cases, you may also be heavily involved in the client allocation calls as the leader if your team is not strong enough to lead them independently.

The recruiting leader is also the master of metrics for the Sprint. I spend the first part of most every day reviewing our dashboards ahead of our standup meetings to ensure I am aware of the progress made. Sometimes I'll ping my team before the call with a snapshot of the metrics and prepare them for critical roles I want to update during our standup. The Sprint Recruiting leader must be data-driven and data-informed to be most effective in this new recruiting framework.

One of the most critical roles the recruiting leader has is to hold everyone to the Sprint Recruiting framework. I find myself redirecting both team members and partners out of the traditional recruiting mindset and back on the principles that make Sprint Recruiting work. Some common questions I find helpful are:
- Why are we focused on a role that was not awarded points this Sprint? Have the priorities changed?
- How are you working during the week using the time blocking method?

- How many points away are we from 100%?
- Are we losing focus on the primary roles identified in this Sprint? If so, why and how do we fix it?

Believe it or not, I usually ask one or all of these questions throughout the Sprint, and we've been doing this for almost two years. I feel like a broken record, but I've found these questions help everyone redirect their focus back to how the client defines success in the sprint-the allocation of points. We'll spend more time discussing the mindset journey for leaders later in the book.

If you would like a template to plan your days and weeks, you can find what I use https://sprintrecruiting.com/wp-content/uploads/2023/04/Leadership-Weekly-Planning.docx.

Product or Sprint Owner

The Sprint Owner (SO) is the key stakeholder for the project. Part of the Sprint Owner's responsibilities is to have a vision of what they wish to build and convey that vision to the scrum team. This is key to successfully starting any Agile software development project. The Agile Sprint Owner does this through the product backlog, a prioritized features list for the product.
Sprint Recruiting would make sense that the executive for a department or line of business would be the Sprint Owner (SO), but we discovered that was not always feasible.

Some department leaders knew very little about the open roles' impacts on their division. Others were still traveling, which made it hard for us to have a bi-weekly allocation call with them.

Sprint Recruiting allows department leaders to designate the SO role to someone on the team who can prioritize work. The owner role requires an individual with specific skills and traits, including availability, proximity to the business needs, and communication skills. The best SOs show commitment by doing whatever is necessary to prioritize the work – and that means being actively engaged with their recruiting partners.

The SO has defined responsibilities in our methodology and must be committed to the success of the Sprint. Be sure to stay away from a SO who tends to consistently blame everyone else for their mistakes, as this will lead to trouble implementing Sprint Recruiting.

Here's a list of their key responsibilities to help you identify the best SO for the job.

- **Define the vision** - The Sprint Owner is the voice of the client and should be able to leverage their high-level perspective to define goals and create a vision for your recruiting team. They are responsible for communicating with stakeholders, including your team, their fellow executives, and hiring managers, to ensure the goals are clear and the vision aligns with business objectives. Having a Sprint Owner with a higher perspective ensures that the team maintains a cohesive vision despite Agile product development's flexible and often fast-paced nature. Everyone needs to be on the same page to work effectively, creating mutual accountability in the recruiting process.
- **Define the Priority** - The key role of the Sprint Owner is to prioritize needs. They must juggle the triangle of scope, budget, and time, weighing priorities according to stakeholders' needs and objectives. The recruiting team should communicate capacity needs or concerns openly with the SO to create a clear set of expectations during the Sprint. The SO takes budgeted points and assigns them to the critical roles in the Sprint. They are also the individuals who can designate a role as expedited since they will have more intimate knowledge of their organization's needs.
- **Providing Feedback** - You will need to be sure your SO is someone comfortable giving feedback, and the more candid, the better. They are your partner in this process, so they need to help you identify ways to become more efficient with every Sprint.
- **Equitable and Firm** -Your Sprint Owner will also need to have a backbone with their peers. They're not only responsible for holding the recruiting team accountable but also the business unit.

They'll be the partner in the Sprint but should not show favoritism through the process. They are the voice of the client but not the ones responsible for giving excuses. If they are to hold you and your team to a definition of success, they keep their department to that same level. It's only when they are as firm with their colleagues as you are with your team that you'll begin to see the real power of this partnership.

Stakeholders

A stakeholder is a broad term to identify key partners in the recruiting process. This could include your HR partners, senior-level executives (not Sprint Owners but maybe their boss), operational support members, or anyone else who plays a role in the recruiting process. The stakeholder involvement will be driven primarily by how you define it.

In the beginning, we involved our HR business partners in our standup and retro meetings. It sounded like a great idea until the team got too big for the meetings to be effective. Some recruiters scheduled weekly huddles with the HRBPs to provide critical updates on the Sprint's progress. Most HRBPs now join the client allocation and retro meetings as stakeholders, which have proven to be a more effective use of everyone's time.

Stakeholders can also include the top line business executive for the group you support. About half of our senior department managers have delegated the allocation of points and day-to-day sprint activities to a designated team member. Although they are not involved in the daily activities, we need to update our senior executives of the progress we make during the Sprint so we will have monthly stakeholder updates with them if needed or required. Believe it or not, many of these executives choose to review the sprint dashboards we have prepared and will schedule a meeting on an as-needed basis.

I would suggest using this [template](https://sprintrecruiting.files.wordpress.com/2023/04/key-roles-worksheet-example.pdf) to begin your thought process. This is a critical part of the planning process and will help ensure a more palatable implementation process. (https://sprintrecruiting.files.wordpress.com/2023/04/key-roles-worksheet-example.pdf)

Key steps in a typical Sprint Recruiting process

There are some new behaviors and norms you will have to train your team and client for. Sprint Recruiting is a predictable process, allowing you and your team to follow a pattern toward success.

Here are some of the key steps you will need to establish in your new process.

Meeting Cadence

Success in Sprint Recruiting is due in part to more frequent and consistent communication. Below is the typical meeting cadence I recommend to clients as they begin implementing the methodology.

If you would like a cheatsheet of the meeting cadences in pdf, click https://sprintrecruiting.files.wordpress.com/2023/04/sprint-recruiting-meeting-cadence-cheatsheet.pdf.

Daily Stand Up

A daily stand up is a short meeting (15 minutes or less) where your team members and Sprint Owner (optional) will come together to share updates on progress towards the goal. This meeting should happen at the same time every day, so it is best to set a priority for scheduling this meeting before any other tasks.

What it is not:
1. A read out of someone's to-dos
2. A forum to solve complex processes or people problems. Take it offline.
3. An optional meeting
4. A place for someone on the team to rant on

The agenda for your stand up goes like this:
1. What progress was made on the roles assigned points?
2. What are the obstacles preventing success?
3. Where does the team member need help?
4. What does the team member commit to doing between now and the next stand up?

Hold to this agenda and it will save you a ton of time and provide you the information you need as a leader to ensure your team succeeds during the sprint.

Your new 101

Do you have regular one-on-one meetings with your employees? If not, you might be missing out on a key opportunity to improve communication and foster a better working relationship. Here are some tips for making the most of your next one-on-one meeting.

Understand the one on one meeting is for your employee, you are there to listen and support
One on one meetings with employees are essential for ensuring a supportive, successful atmosphere in the workplace. During a one

on one, it's important not only to listen to your employee but also to demonstrate your support and commitment to their ongoing development and growth. Giving feedback and offering advice should be done thoughtfully and objectively; additionally, the meeting should provide an opportunity for your employee to express any concerns or issues about which you can lend your assistance. This would be beneficial for both parties; good communication between a manager and an employee not only enhances organizational performance but also increases job satisfaction and morale among staff members.

Set a clear agenda for your one on one.
Setting a clear agenda for the one on one meetings with your employees is key to making sure those meetings are productive. Make sure you include a question about the progress being made on any current projects, and brainstorm together about any obstacles standing in their way that you can help remove. It's also nice to hear what your employees have been learning recently – it shows them that you're taking an interest, as well as making sure they're continuing to stay up to date.

I like to follow the same agenda for every 1o1. Here's what I cover:
- What progress was made on the top 3-5 roles in the sprint according to the points?
- What are any obstacles?
- Where do you need help?
- What will you accomplish this week? Ask for measurable commitments.

If you'd like to use my template, you can download your own version https://sprintrecruiting.files.wordpress.com/2023/04/sprint-recruiting-1o1-agenda-1.docx.

Be open to feedback
Creating an environment in which employees feel comfortable giving honest feedback helps ensure a high-functioning workplace. Regularly encouraging open discussion will help create that

atmosphere and also give you insight into any issues that might need to be addressed in your current management strategy.

Employers should also take this opportunity to receive feedback on their performance and look for areas where they can improve their leadership skills. When implemented consciously, feedback between employers and employees can be effective, empowering, and rewarding for both parties.

Be honest
Being honest with someone when they need improvement is the best way to help them grow. Honesty allows people to pinpoint areas where they may need to practice or gain more experience, avoid repeating mistakes, and progress at a faster rate overall. No one's perfect and it's important to recognize your mistakes and weaknesses in order to develop better skills in the future. By communicating openly and addressing areas of improvement with honesty, you can build stronger relationships and create an atmosphere that values growth and authenticity.

Offer praise and encouragement when appropriate
Praising and encouraging those around you can lead to a healthier work environment, stronger relationships, and improved work-ethic. Praise should be timely and specific – not just general acknowledgments. If your team is working hard to reach a goal, recognize their efforts even if they don't meet the end result. Making incremental successes small causes for celebration, reinforces that there are pros in addition to cons when an effort falls short. Everyone likes to feel appreciated for their work, so showing recognition for all tasks both large and small can serve as an excellent form of motivation for those around you.

If you want to be an effective leader, it's important that you understand what your employees need from you. During this difficult time, many people are struggling and feeling overwhelmed.

As a leader, it's your job to provide support and guidance. By setting a clear agenda for each meeting and being open to feedback, you can create a productive and positive environment for your team. And don't forget to offer praise when it's deserved – everyone likes to feel appreciated.

Biweekly Planning and Retrospective with the client

This is a thirty minute biweekly meeting with your client. The goal is to do a retrospective on what happened in the previous sprint and allocate points for the new one. This may seem like a monumental task but you'll be surprised how quickly the meetings will become as you progress through the Sprint Recruiting methodology. Remember, part of the process is to become more efficient, including your meeting cadence. Also, if you have weekly meetings with hiring managers or other distracting meeting schedules, try to consolidate them into this bi-weekly meeting. It'll save you time and energy but most important, focus, during the sprint.

Here are some ground rules to train your client and make sure you have successful calls from the first sprint.
1.   Everyone comes prepared-It's critical for everyone on the call to be prepared for the call. As you get through your first couple, everyone usually finds their stride and the call runs more efficiently. Hold everyone accountable for planning the discussion ahead of the call which is made easy by having the same three agenda items.
2.   Send your job report ahead of the call- This was another lesson we learned after our second sprint. We leverage google sheets to track all of the open positions at the time the sprint begins. Most of our sprint calls are either Mondays or Tuesdays so we try to have our updates inputted and the report sent out to the POs by noon on Monday beginning a sprint. This helps the POs gather the information they need from their departments to help allocate the points during the call.
3.   Avoid chasing rabbits- Part of the call is designed to discuss and overcome obstacles but do not let this derail your meeting. If a

problem is too complicated to solve on the phone, everyone should agree to take it offline so the call progresses forward.

4.   Document the call and send it to the group-This is a trick I use for every meeting I have but most especially for the sprint calls. A summary email to the group allows everyone to provide feedback and agree to the action items. This is where you capture any obstacles or successes that need more attention with a separate discovery or discussion meeting. It's also great to document the progress of your sprints and hold everyone accountable.

Define The Sprint Workflow

Our team tested several workflows to find what works best. A successful implementation requires you to take as much of the decision making out of the process. It will allow you and your team to focus on meeting your clients' needs. To help you, I'd like to share the sprint workflow we adopted after several iterations. It has helped us turn specific tasks and touch points on auto-pilot and remain focused on filling our pointed positions each sprint. As with everything else in the book, you and your team will need to find what works best for you.

Day 1
•   Meet with the client to complete a retrospective meeting and allocate points for the new sprint.
•   Points are recorded on your report or tracking tool.
•   Recruiters use this information to time-block the next two days of the sprint based on analysis of where they are for each of the positions with points assigned.
•   Emails are sent to the hiring managers who have roles given points alerting them they are "in the spotlight" and set expectations, get availability for interviews, and other needed admin work.
Day 3
•   Recruiters do a quick check-in with the managers active in the sprint to give and receive an update.

- At this point, recruiters should be at or above 50% of their sourcing time block goal for the top 3 roles.
- If candidates have been sourced, this is a good time to do a fly-by with the manager to ensure the recruiter is on track with the sourcing strategy.
- Based on the managers' feedback, recruiters should take some time to block the following two days.

Day 6
- Schedule a quick 15-minute check-in with active sprint job hiring managers to give updates, schedule interviewing blocks, or solicit feedback on interviews.

Day 10
- Recruiters should be 75% through the sourcing time block and approaching above 40% of points budgeted. (If you use 100 points budget, they should be at or above 40 points at this point.)
- Another checkpoint with hiring managers.
- It is a perfect time to provide a quick update to the Sprint Owner/Sprint Owner on the progress and obstacles experienced in the sprint thus far.
- Recruiters should plan and time-block the rest of the sprint.

Day 14
- Day 14 is the final push to close out the sprint and update any reporting tools for accuracy. It is vital to prepare for your retros with your clients and evaluate the sprint's progress as a leader.
- Recruiters should also prepare for the upcoming sprint and get a jumpstart on time-blocking.

One success tip I would share is to book calendar appointments for each of these. Some team members have an hour blocked off on the days listed above to complete the needed tasks to keep the sprint moving towards success.

The commitment to these critical tasks on the assigned days will improve your sprint efficiency, so be sure to discuss with your team what is the best method.

Define Your Points Budgets

One of the questions I get asked most by leaders is "How many points do I give?"

The answer frustrates them because honestly, it's completely up to you. My suggestion is to start with 200 per department as a test. If it is too much or too little, adjust in the next sprint.

Remember, once the points are assigned, do not change them. It will mess with your data integrity if you do.

One key item I did not include in the book is how to advise your partners to allocate their points. This is usually one of the biggest mental obstacles I find when consulting teams. As a result, I built a handy matrix to help guide the conversation and point allocation process.

Impact/Effort Matrix

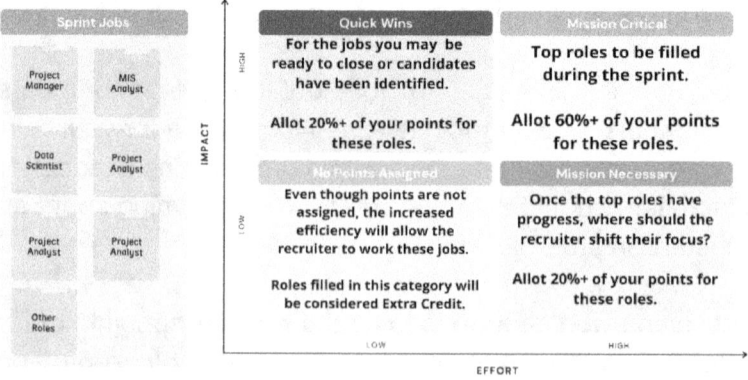

The X-axis represents the amount of effort recruiters will need to use to fill a role. It's divided into high and low. For some, High Effort represents hard to fill jobs because of their niche. For others, it could mean high effort because a ton of applicants have to be screened. The definition is completely up to you.

The Y-axis represents the impact to the business. Again, this is defined by your client, not you. In sales, it could be High Impact if one of the key territories' open sales role isn't filled because it affects revenue.

So, using the matrix, those in the upper right quadrant High Impact and Effort, will need to be allocated 60% of the point budget. Those are Mission Critical roles.

The Quick Wins are assigned 20% of the points. These could be final interviews that happened at the end of the previous sprint that you want to keep your eyes on or roles that you've already identified a qualified talent pool that should be quick fills.

Mission Necessary usually confuses both recruiters and managers. Let's use an example. In this sprint, you have three project analyst roles that are high effort to find but low impact to the client because they really need the Project Manager role filled first.

I have found this helps everyone try to get on the same page when it comes to allocating points.

If you would like a pdf version of the chart above, click here.

WIP Limits

In Sprint Recruiting, WIP limits keep the process moving. Once you're at your limit for a role, you move on to the next one in priority. I've used the example of WIP limits serving like the beat in a song. Every beat keeps the process moving on to the next verse or measure. It's consistent and almost predictable, which allows the listener to focus on the story the song is telling. WIP limits are the beating drum that helps your team quickly evaluate what needs to be done on each role in a priority format.

WIP limits prevent team members from starting tasks on multiple requisitions at the same time. They help your team manage capacity, focus on critical tasks, identify opportunities for continuous improvement, and introduce previously unseen capacity in your process. So say goodbye to the chaotic candy factory and be ready for the new, recruiter controlled rhythmic approach aligned to client expectations but without all of the low-quality outputs, fire drills, and recruiter stress.

During your standup meeting, it's important to review the WIPs with the team to assess better who needs help. It is an opportunity to evaluate the team's current workload and discuss how to move jobs off the board as efficiently as possible. Here are some examples:

- What's closest to being done? What can we do today to move it to "Done"?
- Is anyone working on anything that's not on sprint or doesn't have points assigned?
- Is anything currently blocked from making progress?
- Is anyone available to help move job X to "Done"?

Instead of asking, "What should I work on next?" WIP limits force us to ask, "What can I help move to *Done* before I begin working on another job?"

My recommendation is start with a WIP of 5 in your major recruiting stages and adjust from there.

Measuring and Improving Sprint Recruiting

Now that you have identified the key players, trained your team on the methodology and set up your meeting cadence, there is the issue of measuring and improving your sprints. This requires setting up KPIs (Key Performance Indicators) for each role in the sprint. These can be adjusted depending on different roles or hiring goals throughout the course of a sprint.

Setting up your tracking report

You will need a centralized, virtual report to track the progress of your sprint. This can be as simple as Excel Online, SmartSheet or GoogleSheets. The recruiting team should be able to access the report and update it in real time.
Some key columns you will want to include are:
- Sprint start and end date (separate columns)
- Recruiter
- Job Title
- Date Open
- Days Open
- Hiring Manager
- Points Assigned
- Status (be sure to include DONE)
- Update/Comments for recruiters to provide updates to their managers
- Points Won
- Date closed
- Extra Credit

I created a basic template to provide you the following:

1.   Recruiter Tracking Sheet including the following columns: Recruiter, Sprint Start and End Date, Points Assigned, Points Won, Department, Days Open, TTF
2.   Dashboard including key metrics and graphs to show your progress in the sprint.
You can purchase the template by visiting my online store.

Key Metrics of Sprint

As a reminder from the book, metrics have to be impactful. Be sure your metrics meet the following criteria:
*   *The team uses the metric* – Metrics should not be imposed or measured by management. The metrics should be used voluntarily by Agile teams to learn and improve.
*   *The metric includes conversatio*n – Metrics should not just be numbers. They should be the starting point of a discussion about processes and roadblocks affecting the team. It allows for excellent team buy-in and an opportunity for managers to provide continuous, impactful feedback.
*   *The metric is used in tandem with other metrics* – Even a great metric might lead to tunnel vision if used in a vacuum. It is counterproductive because it will incentivize teams to maximize that metric at the expense of all else. Using several metrics together provides a balanced picture of progress and allows the team to have healthier discussions during the Retrospective meeting.
*   *The metric is easy to calculate and understand* – Metrics that are overly complex or not fully understood, even if they provide useful insights about a team's work, are not valuable for guiding day-to-day activities. So you don't need a report with Vlookups, fancy charts, or interdependent formulas. Please keep it simple but measurable.

Now let's dive into some of the metrics you will measure in Sprint Recruiting.

Points Assigned vs Points Won

You'll need to show how many points were obtained during the sprint and how many remain. It helps the team celebrate the wins but identify what gaps remain. During the stand-up meetings, it is helpful to provide some clarity for what tasks need to be accomplished before the next meeting. This chart makes it instantly clear how much value has already been delivered and how close the team is to meeting its commitment for that sprint.

I use this chart daily to measure our progress and determine if we are on track to meet our client's definition of success. The simplicity of the chart allows sprint participants to understand some important metrics and assumptions quickly.

To set up this chart, you will need to calculate the following into a pivot table:
- Total points assigned (sum of column)
- Total points won (sum of column)
- Total extra credit (sum of column)

Create a Bar/Line graph with the bar representing the total points assigned and the points won and extra credit represented by lines. This view will show you each sprint, how you and the team performed. Here's what it should look like:

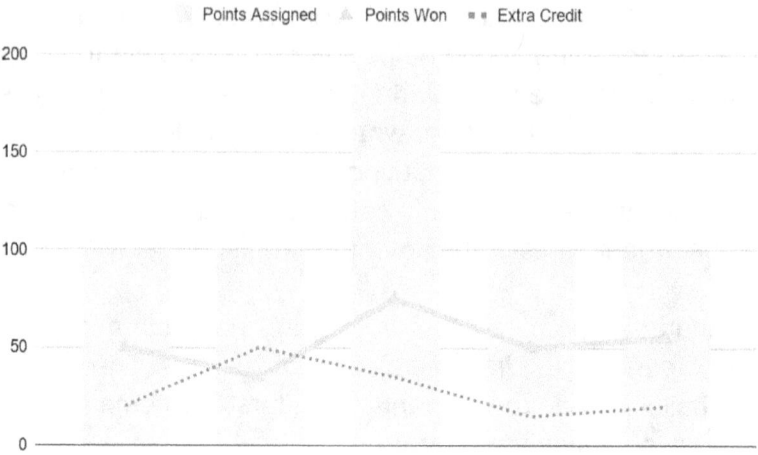

Points Assigned versus Points Won

Points Assigned   Points Won   Extra Credit

Open versus Hired Chart

Remember, the mindset shift from traditional to Sprint Recruiting takes a while. You will not be able to convince your clients or even your team to let go of the only metrics they've known. Tracking the open versus hired sprint to sprint will help with the adoption process while also showing the Sprint Recruiting value.

Leverage the open versus hired report as a contrast to the new values of Sprint Recruiting. We found once our clients began embracing the point system, the open versus hired report began to show more positive trends. We used this data to prove why the new methodology was more productive.

As the business starts prioritizing positions, and your team uses this focus to create efficiencies, the byproduct is the ability to fill more jobs within two weeks. Without charting the progress, you will miss out on a critical tool to help transition out of the old and into the new way of thinking.

Points by Status

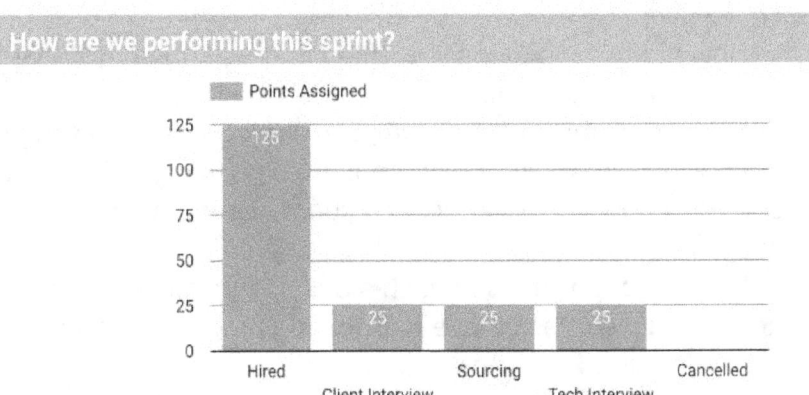

This is a vital part of my metric dashboard. I want to know daily how many points we have in each stage of the process. Depending on what day of the sprint I am looking at, this data can help me know whether it's smooth sailing towards a great sprint or if I'm heading into a potential storm.

Other Key Metrics to Consider

My dashboard "favorites" are based on the Sprint Recruiting Methodology. Here are a couple of metrics I track on my dashboard:

- Average time open. I usually have this in a numeric banner over a pie chart breaking the metrics down into categories: <30 days, <45 days, 45+ days.
- Funnel Metrics
  - How many candidates in recruiter screening versus the number of openings? I typically like to see the number of screenings at or above 2.5 times the number of roles.

- How many candidates in a technical interview? This is the next stage in the funnel so I want to have 1.5 times the number of roles in this step.
- How many candidates in a hiring manager interview? For this stage, I use 1.5 as well.
- I also track this in a day over day chart to measure progress and anticipate issues before they happen. Over time, you learn to almost predict how you will end each sprint based on the numbers reported.
- Number of positions in each stage: Sourcing, Screening, Interview, etc. I also track these daily to see progress and where I need to dig in during my one on ones.
- Number of positions by department and/or client
- Trending time to fill over the last 90 days
- Pipeline statistics: I am a huge proponent of having a pipeline of vetted candidates ready for roles when they open. My dashboard shows how many we have in each pool and the last touchpoint.

Candidate satisfaction

Assessing candidate satisfaction is a great way to understand how successful your hiring process truly is. To gauge their opinion of the experience, employers often seek feedback from candidates through surveys. Key questions you should ask include: Did we offer an accurate description of the role? Was communication efficient and effective? Did any issues arise during the recruitment period - if so, what were they?

Why is it valuable?

It's clear that the candidate experience is becoming a key priority for talent acquisition leaders. As an example, recruiters at A.P Moller-Maersk are learning how to interact with candidates in order to offer a transparent and authentic representation of their company culture. Similarly, Selfridges has added more personal interactions so applicants feel appreciated - it's all about the human touch!

Employers must pay more attention than ever to their reputation, as the growth of employer review sites and social media have made it easy for job seekers to share negative experiences. Studies reveal that when a candidate has had an unpleasant experience with a company they will not only leave but also broadcast this information widely.

By keeping tabs on candidate satisfaction you can identify any issues quickly and make the necessary changes in order to turn them around.

Cost per hire

To calculate the cost of new hires for your organization, simply add up all related expenses from a given period and divide that sum by the total number of recruitments during said time frame. These expenditures may include salaries paid to recruiting team members, fees charged by staffing companies and advertising costs.

Cost per hire became less important in recent years amid a fierce battle for talent. As the economic climate continues to evolve, cost per hire has become a necessary metric once more. The price can be quite substantial - as high as $4,700 according to SHRM - so recruiting leaders must show they are taking all necessary measures to keep expenses at bay.

The initial step to reducing cost-per-hire is assessing your expenses with the help of American National Standards Institute's [ANSI] metric for ascertaining cost per hire. It's a wise decision to identify where you are investing substantially and explore ways that won't affect performance while cutting back costs.

Take this opportunity, as well, to develop your talent pipeline if hiring has been slowed down currently; use it judiciously in order to build connections with prospective candidates. Making acquaintances broadens your network immensely and minimizes expenditure on finding applicants when recruitment begins again!

Candidate Diversity

If you wish to evaluate your recruitment and selection process' efficacy in terms of diversity, Candidate Diversity Metrics can provide valuable insight. This assessment takes into account the breadth of potential job applicants from underrepresented groups, as well as their respective sources, taking a multi-faceted approach which includes analyzing the pool via various metrics such as those pertaining to who is hired for a given role.

As a growing number of employers come to recognize it, diversity in hiring is not only the right thing to do but also presents significant benefits for their business. Studies have shown that companies with varied workforces tend to outperform those without; on top of this, job seekers will often take into account an employer's commitment to workforce diversification when considering employment opportunities.

To advance diversity and inclusion, it is essential to track its metrics. As Joan C. Williams and Jamie Dolkas stated in the Harvard Business Review, employers need a "metrics-based approach" that can reveal issues, establish benchmarks, and evaluate progress for it to be successful.

It is important for employers to understand that the success of diversity and inclusion initiatives depends on the engagement of their employees, who should feel empowered to provide feedback.

Employers need to create an environment where all employees are treated with respect and can feel safe expressing their opinions and ideas. Tools such as anonymous surveys, focus groups, or even team activities can help employers assess how well their initiatives are being received and implemented.

Hiring manager experience

To measure the success of your sourcing and vetting services, consider implementing a hiring manager satisfaction metric. This will help you gain insight into how satisfied managers are with all that you do! Keep in mind, this is an entirely subjective assessment based on surveys--not numerical figures or metrics.

Your survey will include questions for hiring managers to rate you on your comprehension of the job prerequisites, the caliber of potential employees presented, and how rapidly and effectively you responded. I also like to provide as many qualitative data points as quantitative. The qualitative data helps me better understand the scores and will often help recruiting leaders devise success strategies to improve critical points in the hiring process. Nurturing strong connections with hiring managers is indispensable; the collaboration between recruiters and hiring managers has been described as the most significant factor in talent acquisition success. The top-notch recruiters, claims Josh Bersin – Global Industry Analyst and Founder of The Josh Bersin Company – "establish solid relationships with their respective Hiring Managers while being completely aware of the requirements for which they are recruiting."

For recruiting leaders who want to be seen as trusted allies and strategic advisors, developing a strong collaboration with hiring managers is essential. Rather than simply following orders from the higher-ups, you should demonstrate that you understand their business objectives and aid in selecting strategies for staffing decisions. It's also a great way to let your primary client know you're listening and iterating the process to better meet their needs.

Visualizing the Data

Let's go through some examples of how I like to display data.

As mentioned, there are different metrics I track using the Sprint Recruiting methodology. The first metric I have on my dashboard is the number of points won versus number of points assigned. This shows me how the team is performing against how the client defined priority during the sprint.

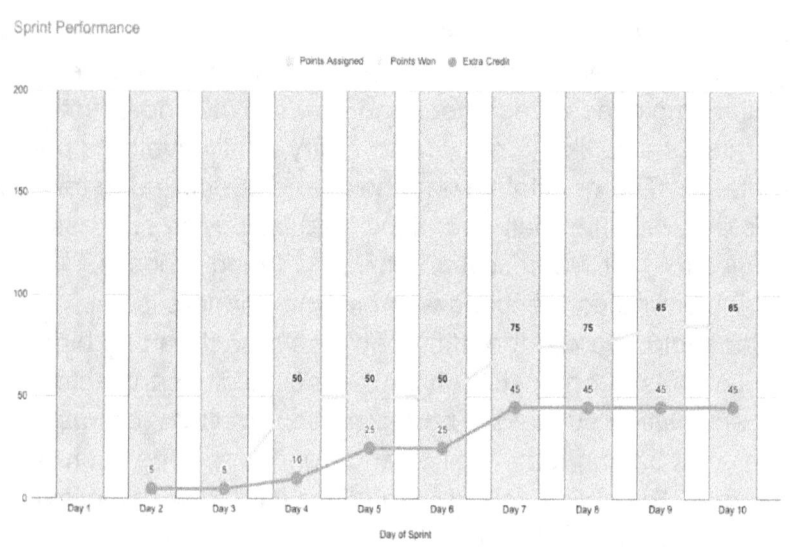

I use this chart daily to measure our progress and determine if we are on track to meet our client's definition of success. The simplicity of the chart allows sprint participants to understand some important metrics and assumptions quickly:

- The chart shows the team usually begins closing roles on the fifth day of the sprint and again on day 8 and 9. If this is my baseline of performance, I'll be able to diagnose performance of future sprints, almost by the day. This is a vital insight I use several times throughout the day.

- Notice the points won and extra credit. The "extra credit" points are points given to additional roles filled that were not identified as priority during our two week sprint. The goal for Sprint Recruiting is to track all work and reallocate focus and resources based on the data. This particular line compared to the "points won " line enables me to quickly identify if either 1. the clients are changing priority in the sprint or 2. recruiters are filling easy jobs versus those identified as priority. Either way, it's a valuable insight into the team's performance.

The Sprint Burndown Chart is one of the most critical tools you will use throughout the sprint. Its simplicity allows sprint participants to improve performance with the passing of each sprint. As a leader, it will be the chart you use to determine gaps in the recruiting delivery process. Recruiters can quickly assess their ability to meet the needs of the client.

Clients will use it to understand their part in the success of a successful sprint.

Performance Snapshot	
# Open	On Hold
17	0
Hires	Offers
4	0
PS Goal	Pre-Screen
42.5	46
TIV Goal	Tech Interview
25.5	9
CIV Goal	Client Interview
25.5	21

Another critical section of my dashboard tracks the lead and lag measures for the sprint. As an example, the Performance Snapshot in this diagram tells me our funnel is a little weak in the technical interview (TIV) part of the process. We have a lot of candidates at the top of the funnel and enough meetings with clients (CIV) but without at least 25 candidates active in TIV, we may not hit our goal by the end of the sprint.

I cannot express the importance of tracking your key lead measures daily. Waiting for the end of a sprint or the end of a month to address activities needed to meet your goals is useless. I like to have this on my first page of the dashboard so I can relate the activities/lead measures against the performance in the first chart discussed.

Both charts are interesting but become impactful when combined.

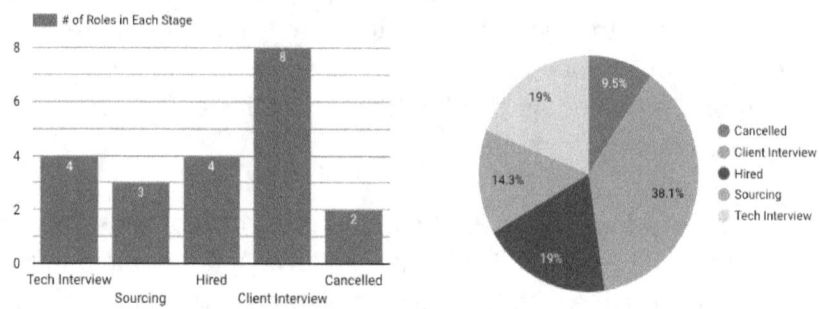

I like to see how many jobs are in each stage of the process represented both numerically and as a percentage. This is an example of how two charts showing the same information can provide another viewpoint. In this example, if the Client Interview is my last stage before hiring, 38% of my roles in this category could be a good thing. This is highly dependent on what day of the sprint as well.

If this metric is on Day 2, that's great. If it's on Day 8, it may not be as favorable.

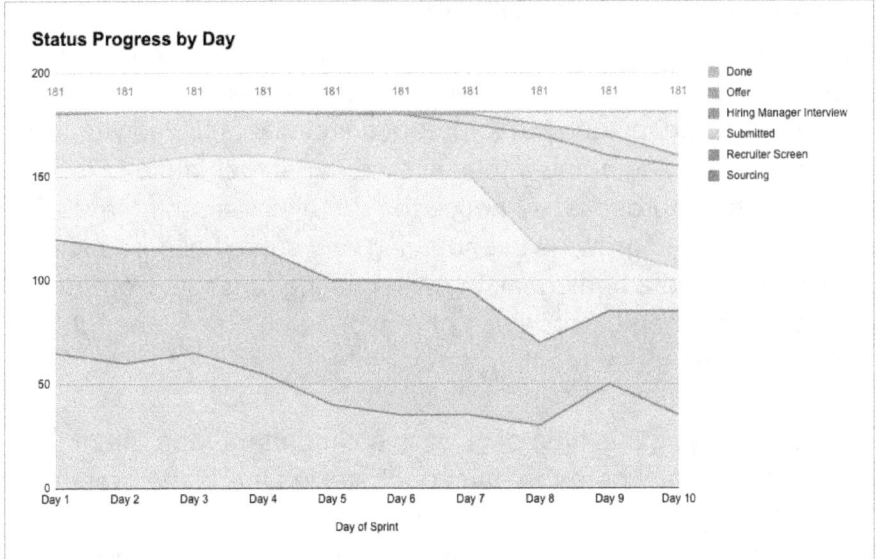

Another viewpoint is to track the change in status daily. An area chart is a great way to display this type of information. In this example, I am tracking how the team moves requisition statuses by day for 181 positions. The area chart shows how positions move through the process and allows leaders to identify the common workflow of positions as a whole. This chart can be confusing for some but it just takes a little getting used to.

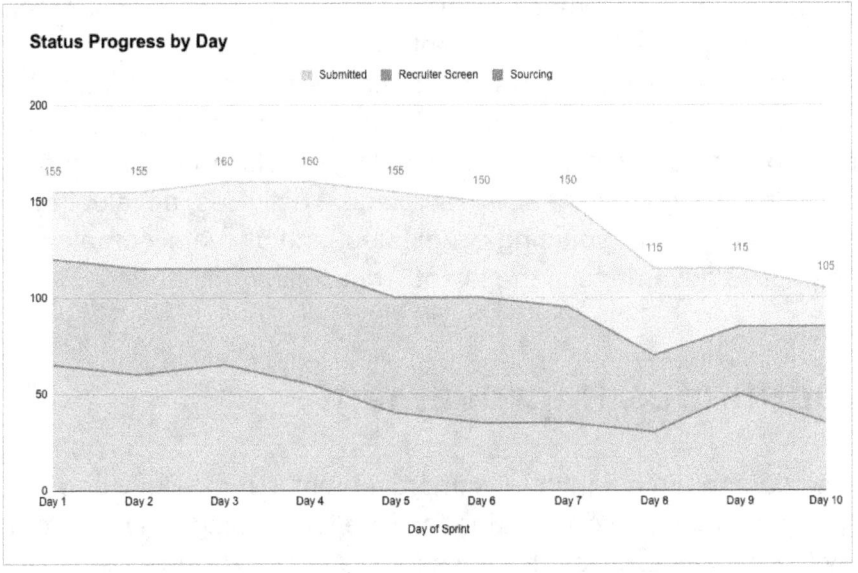

Let's say I want to focus on the top of the funnel or the categories known by sourcing, recruiter screens and submittals. Stripping the other components of the chart allows me to focus on how many roles need to be in sourcing to produce submittals. I also want to review the average number jobs in recruiter screening to understand the process. If I notice the recruiter screening area (the middle) begins to grow as the sourcing and submittal areas shrink, it tells me I have a bottleneck in my recruiting function. Perhaps they have too many screenings or maybe I don't have enough recruiters to do the screening.

This is why using this type of chart is so important for a talent leader to identify where the gaps or obstacles are in the process.

If you'd like a handy tool to begin your preparations, be sure to visit: https://sprintrecruiting.files.wordpress.com/2023/04/measure-what-counts.pdf.

Last thing about Data

Measuring the performance of your recruitment team is critical for success. Recruiting metrics provide insight into how well your team is performing, enabling you to identify areas of opportunity and make changes that could result in a more effective recruitment process. Tracking these metrics allows you to optimize processes and maximize the value of your recruiting efforts, improving quality of hire, reducing time spent on recruitment activities, developing better strategies for sourcing candidates, and ultimately creating a competitive advantage in the talent landscape.

Continuous Improvement

Using data to force continuous improvement is most likely one of my favorite things to do as a leader. The funnel diagram is a great way to start this process. It allows for me to quickly view the progress of each stage and compare it against internal goals. I can easily visualize what areas are strong and which need improvement, as well as identify any bottlenecks that may be limiting performance.

Combining lead measures with key performance indicators (KPIs) gives me the best of both worlds. This helps me to identify trends and develop strategies for improvement, ensuring that my team is always improving its processes and maximizing value. With this data-driven approach, I can make sure that my recruitment effort is constantly working towards greater efficiency.

The ability to track KPIs and lead measures in real-time is also highly valuable. This gives me the ability to quickly adapt and make changes if necessary, while also keeping me on track with my goals. With accurate data, I can monitor progress in a timely manner so that any needed adjustments are made quickly and accurately.

Regular review of the KPIs allows me to ensure that my team is staying on target and also helps me identify any potential issues that may arise. Monitoring lead measures provides me with the insights to make necessary changes quickly, allowing for quicker improvement and higher success rates in recruitment.

Overall, tracking key performance indicators is essential to evaluate your team's performance, while also providing you with the data needed to drive continuous improvement.

Conclusion

- Summary of key takeaways
- Common objections to Sprint Recruiting
- Final Q&A session
- Action plan for implementing Sprint Recruiting in the participant's organization.

Key Takeaways

Implementing a new recruiting process and methodology will be tough. It will require a change in mindset, processes and resources. It is important for organizations to be prepared to make a commitment to the process and be ready to invest in any new resources that may be necessary.
If you want to survive and thrive in this new era of talent acquisition, there are some lessons to learn from history's most successful military leaders.

Warrior Leadership is a powerful, motivational, and distinctive style of leadership that, when studied and properly applied, will produce the results you want in your company. True warrior leaders have shared goals with their unit: defense, growth, service, and the purpose to make things better for everyone involved. They lead not from a throne but in the midst of their team. Warrior leaders are brave enough to stand on the front lines with a confidence that generates hope for all on the team. From this, a sense of authority is born naturally and conferred on the leader.

Mike Hayes, former commanding officer of Navy SEAL Team TWO and author, says the key to warrior leadership is to "push to the limits across many different dimensions – we can never be strong enough, never focused enough, never patient enough, never accountable enough." In his book, "Never Enough: A Navy SEAL

Commander on Living a Life of Excellence, Agility, and Meaning", Hayes uses stories to teach what it means to lead one of the most highly trained and successful military teams.

Here are some of the traits of a successful Warrior Leader for you to consider.

Choose the hard path.

One of my personal mottos at work for me and the teams I lead has been "Excellence Always". It has been a core value because it sets the tone for a mindset of continuous improvement and never being satisfied with normal. If you were to analyze the most successful military units, you would find them being led by effective leaders who push themselves and their teams to choose the hard path. The leaders tend to spend more time focusing on outcomes, not outputs.

This does not mean you take unnecessary risks. Warrior leaders understand the need for and have experience with pushing the team towards calculated risks. These are risks that will stretch and evolve the team but not set them up for failure.

Embrace the Suck

If you've watched the movie 300 or studied the Battle of Thermopylae, the leader Leonidas and his soldiers knew the battle they were walking into. It was going to be a hard, long fight to protect Greece long enough to prepare for the Persian invasion. Their mission was to stall the enemy. Those in his army were experienced enough to know they were walking into a potential slaughter but they pressed forward. The call of honor was greater than the "suck" they were about to face.

I once heard a speaker who was former military discuss how he pushed his team to embrace the suck. He noted most of the time when we feel there is no way to push forward, the real opportunity for growth is just on the other side of the "suck". I know personally, when working out, when I push beyond what I call the "suck limit", I can do more repetitions or more weight than my willpower had me believe I could.

It's easy to show the best sides of ourselves when faced with obstacles we are confident we can handle but it's harder when we're pushed beyond our perceived or self-imposed limits. Through continually improving our emotional intelligence, we can enhance self-awareness and control our emotions in the most challenging of circumstances.

The more you push comfort zone expansion the more you, and your teams, gain the strength, experience and foresight to navigate adversity.

Balance confidence and extreme humility

Perhaps one of the harder traits to balance is the important duality of leadership. Warrior Leaders have to think slow and fast, serve others before themselves, and apply feedback for making continual improvements. You want to have the confidence to inspire your team but maintain the humility that will allow them to feel safe coming to you. This is a struggle most of us battle daily with some days being better than others.

Being a leader is tough, being a Talent Leader is becoming more and more challenging. Keep your head up and lean on fellow leaders who, believe it or not, are struggling with the same battles!

Common Objections to Sprint Recruiting

I have implemented this methodology in three organizations as a leader and many more as a consultant. Here are some of the common objections I hear and how I tend to overcome them.

1. Lack of time: Some companies may feel that they are too busy to implement Sprint Recruiting. They may believe that taking the time to plan and execute Sprint Recruiting will take away from other important tasks and projects. The truth is this new way of recruiting will improve speed to hire along with candidate quality and experience. Leaders who value top talent will understand the time implementing and adjusting to Sprint Recruiting will be an investment.

2. Resistance to change: Many organizations are resistant to change, particularly when it comes to established recruiting practices. Some hiring managers may feel that they have a system that works, and they may be hesitant to try something new. There is no guarantee that Sprint Recruiting will be successful. But by taking the time to understand each team and what they need, leaders can increase their chances of finding top talent through a more efficient process. Additionally, with careful planning and feedback loops in place, any changes that need to be made after implementation can quickly be identified and addressed.

3. Lack of buy-in: Leaders may be unable to secure the necessary support for Sprint Recruiting from stakeholders, team members or other departments. It's important to ensure that all involved are aware of how this method will benefit the company by improving speed to hire, candidate quality and experience.

4. Uncertainty about results: Implementing a new recruiting process can be risky, and some companies may be hesitant to take on that risk. They may want to see evidence that Sprint Recruiting can produce better results before committing to it. This is why starting with a small group as a test is so important. Once you're able to get through two successful sprints, they will become your internal cheerleaders.

5. Lack of resources: Sprint Recruiting requires a significant investment of time and resources, particularly in terms of training and software. Some companies may not have the resources to commit to this kind of initiative. In traditional models, there is a

difficulty in coordinating teams. Sprint Recruiting requires close coordination between recruiters and hiring managers, which can be challenging for some organizations. Some may struggle to align schedules and communication between different teams.

Have a Sprint Zero

Before you dive headlong into Sprint Recruiting with your client, it's a good idea to have a sprint 0. In this sprint, you and your team can assign points to requisitions you feel are most important to the client and begin testing the framework and reporting before going live. Our first two sprints were without client involvement during our beta versions of Sprint Recruiting. It allowed us to test several aspects of Sprint Recruiting before going full-on with the client and creating more issues than we needed to manage.

Once you've assigned your fake points to the roles, begin conducting your daily stand-ups with the team, focusing on the roles assigned points. Sprint 0 is a great way to help your team get used to only discussing updates and obstacles for the sprint roles. Our team had a hard time staying on track initially, but as we began holding each other accountable, our meetings became more effective. It helped us grow closer as a team and identify any mindset shifts we needed to address before going live with our client.

Here are some helpful steps to remember as you begin your Sprint 0 journey:

1.   **Define Clear Goals and Objectives**: Before starting Sprint 0, it's important to define clear goals and objectives for the sprint. These goals could include establishing the project vision, defining the product backlog, creating a sprint backlog, and setting up the reporting environment. Having well-defined goals and objectives helps the team stay focused and aligned throughout the sprint.

2.   **Create a Detailed Plan**: Plan out the activities and tasks that need to be accomplished during Sprint 0. This includes creating a timeline, identifying resources, assigning responsibilities, and setting deadlines. A detailed plan helps the team stay organized and ensures that everyone knows what is expected of them during the sprint.

3.   **Establish Communication Channels**: Communication is key in Sprint Recruiting, so it's important to establish effective communication channels during Sprint 0. This includes setting up regular team meetings (refer to the Meeting Cadence document), defining communication protocols, and establishing a system for tracking progress and reporting issues. Clear communication channels facilitate collaboration and ensure that everyone is on the same page.

4.   **Define Practices and Workflows**: Define the practices and workflows that will be followed during the sprint. This includes establishing the sprint length, defining the roles and responsibilities of team members, setting up daily stand-up meetings, and establishing the process for backlog refinement, sprint planning, sprint reviews, and sprint retrospectives. Clearly defined practices and workflows help the team follow a standardized approach and ensure smooth execution of the sprint.

Remember, Sprint 0 is a planning phase that sets the foundation for the rest of the project. Taking the time to properly set up Sprint 0 can greatly contribute to the success of Sprint Recruiting in your organization.

Best Wishes

If you've made it to the end of this document and performed the necessary assessments and tasks, you're ready to become a Sprint Recruiting Leader! It takes time, focus and commitment to make it work. But with the right attitude, tools and processes in place, you can find your team gaining momentum quickly. Best of luck!

Resources:

101 Agenda:
https://sprintrecruiting.files.wordpress.com/2023/04/sprint-recruiting-1o1-agenda-1.docx

Benefits of Sprint Recruiting Deck
https://sprintrecruiting.files.wordpress.com/2023/04/the-benefits-of-sprint-recruiting-.pdf

Leadership Mindset Planning
https://sprintrecruiting.files.wordpress.com/2023/04/sprint-recruitingleader-mindset-preparation.pdf

Sprint Recruiting Job Template
https://sprintrecruiting.files.wordpress.com/2023/04/the-sprint-recruiter-job-profile.pdf

Key Sprint Roles Worksheet
https://sprintrecruiting.files.wordpress.com/2023/04/key-roles-worksheet-example.pdf

Meeting Cadence
https://sprintrecruiting.files.wordpress.com/2023/04/sprint-recruiting-meeting-cadence-cheatsheet.pdf

Measure What Counts
https://sprintrecruiting.files.wordpress.com/2023/04/measure-what-counts.pdf

Point Allocation Matrix
https://sprintrecruiting.files.wordpress.com/2023/04/sprint-recruiting-santander-1.pdf

www.ingramcontent.com/pod-product-compliance
Lightning Source LLC
Chambersburg PA
CBHW062248290526
45794CB00006B/2451